"Three Days to See"

was published in

Atlantic Monthly

in January, 1933

written by Helen Keller

"Three Days to See"

ONE

All of us have read thrilling stories in which the hero had only a limited and specified time to live. Sometimes it was as long as a year; sometimes as short as twenty-four hours. But always we were interested in discovering just how the doomed man chose to spend his last days or his last hours. I speak, of course, of free men who have a choice, not condemned criminals whose sphere of activities is strictly delimited.

Such stories set us thinking, wondering what we should do under similar circumstances. What events, what experiences, what associations, should we crowd into those last hours as mortal beings? What happi-

ness should we find in reviewing
the past, what regrets?

Sometimes I have thought it
would be an excellent rule to live
each day as if we should die tomorrow. Such an attitude would em-
phasize sharply the values of life.
We should live each day with a
gentleness, a vigor, and a keen-
ness of appreciation which are often lost when time stretches before
us in the constant panorama of
more days and months and years to
come. There are those, of course,
who would adopt the epicurean
motto of 'Eat, drink, and be merry,'
but most people would be chasten-
ed by the certainty of impending
death.

In stories, the doomed hero is
usually saved at the last minute
by some stroke of fortune, but
almost always his sense of values

is changed. He becomes more appreciative of the meaning of life and its permanent spiritual values. It has often been noted that those who live, or have lived, in the shadow of death bring a mellow sweetness to everything they do.

Most of us, however, take life for granted. We know that one day we must die, but usually we picture that day as far in the future. When we are in buoyant health, death is all but unimaginable. We seldom think of it. The days stretch out in an endless vista. So we go about our petty tasks, hardly aware of our listless attitude toward life.

The same lethargy, I am afraid, characterizes the use of all our facilities and senses. Only the deaf appreciate hearing, only the blind realize the manifold blessings that lie in sight. Particularly does this observation apply to those who have lost sight and hearing in adult life. But those who have never suffered impairment of sight or hearing seldom make the fullest use of these blessed faculties. Their eyes and ears take in all sights and sounds hazily, without concentration and with little appreciation. It is the same old story of not being grateful for what we have until we lose it, of not being conscious of health until we are ill.

I have often thought it would be a blessing if each human being were stricken blind and deaf for a few days at some time during his early adult life. Darkness would make him more appreciative of sight; silence would teach him the joys of sound.

Now and then I have tested my seeing friends to discover what they see. Recently I was visited by a very good friend who had just returned from a long walk in the woods, and I asked her what she had observed. 'Nothing in particular,' she replied. I might have been incredulous had I not been accustomed to such responses, for long ago I became convinced that the seeing see little.

How was it possible, I asked myself, to walk for an hour through the woods and see nothing worthy of note? I who cannot see find hundreds of things to interest me through mere touch. I feel the delicate symmetry of a leaf. I pass my hands lovingly about the smooth skin of a silver birch, or the rough, shaggy bark of a pine. In spring I touch the branches of trees hopefully in search of a bud, the first sign of awakening Nature after her winter's sleep. I feel the delightful, velvety texture of a flower, and discover its remarkable convolutions; and something of the miracle of Nature is revealed to me. Occasionally, if I am very fortunate, I place my hand gently on a small tree and feel the happy quiver of a bird in full song. I am delighted to have the cool waters of a brook rush through my open fingers. To me a lush carpet of pine needles or spongy grass is more welcome than the most luxurious Persian rug. To me the pageant of seasons is a thrilling and unending drama, the action of which streams through my finger tips.

At times my heart cries out with longing to see all these things. If I can get so much pleasure from mere touch, how much more beauty must be revealed by sight. Yet, those who have eyes apparently see little. The panorama of color and action which fills the world is taken for granted. It is human, perhaps, to appreciate little that which have and to long for that which we have not, but it is a great pity that in the world of light the gift of sight is used only as a mere convenience rather than as a means of adding fullness to life.

If I were the president of a university I should establish a compulsory course in 'How to Use Your Eyes'. The professor would try to show his pupils how they could add joy to their lives by really seeing what passes unnoticed before them. He would try to awake their dormant and sluggish faculties.

TWO

Perhaps I can best illustrate by imagining what I should most like to see if I was given the use of my eyes, say, for just three days. And while I am imagining, suppose you, too, set your mind to work on the problem of how you would use your own eyes if you had only three days to see. If with the on-coming darkness if the third night you knew that the sun would never rise for you again, how would you spend those three inter-vening days? What would you most want to let your gaze rest upon?

I, naturally, should want most to see the things which have be-come dear to me through my years of darkness. You, too, would want to let your eyes rest long on the things that have become

dear to you so that you could take
the memory of them with you into
the night that loomed before you.

If, by some miracle, I were
granted three seeing days, to be
followed by a relapse into darkness, I should divide the period
into three parts.

On the first day, I should want
to see the people whose kindness
and gentleness and companionship
have made my life worth living.
First I should like to gaze long
upon the face of my dear teacher,
Mrs. Ann Sullivan Macy, who
came to me when I was a child and
opened the outer world to me. I
should want not merely to see the
outline of her face, so that I
could cherish it in my memory,
but to study that face and find in
it the living evidence of the sym-
pathetic tenderness and patience

9

with which she accomplished the difficult task of my education. I should like to see in her eyes that strength of character which has enabled her to stand firm in the face of difficulties, and that compassion for all humanity which she has revealed to me so often.

I do not know what it is to see into the heart of a friend through that 'window of the soul,' the eye. I can only 'see' through my finger tips the outline of a face. I can detect laughter, sorrow, and many other obvious emotions. I know my friends from the feel of their faces. But I cannot really picture their personalities, of course, through the thoughts they express to me, through whatever of their actions are revealed to me. But I am denied that deeper understanding of them which I am sure would come through sight of

them, through watching their reactions to various expressed and circumstances, through noting the im-
mediate and fleeting reactions of
their eyes and countenance.

Friends who are near to me I
know well, because through the
months and years they reveal themselves to me in all their phases; but
of casual friends I have only an
incomplete impression, an impression gained from handclasp, from
spoken words which I take from
their lips with my finger tips, or
which they tap into the palm of my
hand.

How much easier, how much more
satisfying it is for you who can see
to grasp quickly the essential quali-
ties of another person by watching
the subtleties of expression, the
quiver of a muscle, the flutter of a
hand. But does it ever occur to you

to use your sight to see the inner nature of a friend or acquaintance? Do not most of you seeing people grasp casually the outward features of a face and let it go at that?

For instance, can you describe accurately the faces of five good friends? Some of you can, but many cannot. As an experiment, I have questioned husbands of long standing about the color of their wives' eyes, and often they express embarrassed confusion and admit that they so not know. And, incidentally, it is a chronic complaint of wives that their husbands do not notice new dresses, new hats, and changes in household arrangements.

The eyes of seeing persons soon become accustomed to the routine of their surroundings, and they actually see only the startling and spectacular. But even in viewing

the most spectacular sights the
eyes are lazy. Court records reveal
every day how inaccurately 'eye-
witnesses' see. A given event will
be 'seen' in several different ways
by as many witnesses. Some see
more than others, but few see everything that is within the range
of their vision.

Oh, the things that I should see
if I had the power of sight for just
three days!

The first day would be a busy
one. I should call to me all my dear
friends and look long into their
faces, imprinting upon my mind the
outward evidence of the beauty that
is within them. I should let my eyes
rest, too, on the face of a baby, so
that I could catch a vision of the
eager, innocent beauty which pre-
cedes the individuals consciousness
of the conflicts which life develops.

13

And I should like to look into
the loyal, trusting eyes of my dogs
– the grave, canny little Scottie,
Darkie, and the stalwart, understanding Great Dane, Helga, whose
warm, tender, and playful friend-
ships are so comforting to me.

On that busy first day I should
also view the small simple things
of my home. I want to see the
warm colors in the rugs under my
feet, the pictures on the walls, the
intimate trifles that transform a
house into a home. My eyes would
rest respectfully on the books in
raised type which I have read, but
they would be more eagerly interested in the printed books which
seeing people can read, for during
the long night of my life the books
I have read and those which have
been read to me have built themselves into a great shining light-
house, revealing to me the deepest

channels of human life and the
human spirit.

In the afternoon of that first
seeing day, I should take a long
walk in the woods and intoxicate
my eyes on the beauties of the
world of Nature, trying desperate-
ly to absorb in a few hours the
vast splendor which is constantly
unfolding itself to those who can
see. On the way home from my
woodland jaunt my path would lie
near a farm so that I might see the
patient horses ploughing in the
field (perhaps I should see only a
tractor!) and the serene content of
men living close to the soil. And I
should pray for the glory of a
colorful sunset.

When dusk had fallen, I should
experience the double delight of
being able to see by artificial light,
which the genius of man has created

15

to extend the power of his sight
when Nature decrees darkness.

In the night of that first day of
sight, I should not be able to sleep,
so full would be my mind of the
memories of the day.

THREE

The next day - the second day
of sight - I should arise with the
dawn and see the thrilling miracle
by which night is transformed into day. I should behold with awe
the magnificent panorama of light
with which the sun awakens the
sleeping earth.

This day I should devote to a
hasty glimpse of the world, past
and present. I should want to see
the pageant of man's progress, the

kaleidoscope of the ages. How can
so much compressed into one day?
Through the museums, of course.
Often I have visited the New York
Museum of Natural History to
touch with my hands many of the
objects there exhibited, but I have
longed to see with my eyes the
condensed history of the earth and
its inhabitants displayed there -
animals and the races of men pictured in their native environment;
gigantic carcasses of dinosaurs and
mastodons which roamed the earth
long before man appeared, with his
tiny stature and powerful brain, to
conquer the animal kingdom; realis-
tic presentations of the processes
of evolution in animals, and in the
implements which man has used to
fashion for himself a secure home
on this planet; and a thousand and
one other aspects of natural history.

I wonder how many readers of
this article have viewed this panorama of the face of living things
as pictured in that inspiring
museum. Many, of course, have
not had the opportunity, but, I
am sure that many who have had
the opportunity have not made
use of it. There, indeed, is a place
to use your eyes. You who can see
can spend many fruitful days
there, but I, with my imaginary
three days of sight, could only
take a hasty glimpse, and pass on.

My next stop would be the Metropolitan Museum of Art, for
just as the Museum of Natural
History reveals the material aspects of the world, so does the
Metropolitan show the myriad
facets of the human spirit.
Throughout the history of humanity the urge to artistic expression has been almost as powerful

as the urge for food, shelter, and procreation. And here, in the vast chambers of the Metropolitan Museum, is unfolded before me the spirit of Egypt, Greece, and Rome, as expressed in their art. I know well through my hands the sculptured gods and goddesses of the ancient Nile-land. I have a few copies of Parthenon friezes, and I have sensed the rhythmic beauty of charging Athenian warriors. Apollos and Venuses and the winged victory of Samothrace are friends of my finger tips. The gnarled, bearded features of Homer are dear to me, for he, too, knew blindness.

My hands have lingered upon the living marvel of Roman sculpture as well as that of later generations. I have passed my hands over a plaster cast of Michelangelo's inspiring and heroic Moses; I have sensed the power of Rodin; I

have been awed by the devoted
spirit of Gothic wood carving.
These arts which can be touched
have meaning for me, but even
they were meant to be seen rather
than felt, and I can only guess at
the beauty which remains hidden
from me. I can admire the simple
lines of a Greek vase, but its
figured decorations are lost to me.

So on this, my second day of
sight, I should try to probe into
the soul of man through his art.
The things I knew through touch
I should now see. More splendid
still, the whole magnificent world
of painting would be opened to
me, from the Italian Primitives,
with their serene religious devot-
ion, to the Moderns, with their
feverish visions. I should look
deep into the canvases of Raphael,
Leonardo Da Vinci, Titian, Rem-
brandt. I should want to feast my

eyes upon the warm colors of Veronese, study the mysteries of El Greco, catch a new vision of Nature from Corot. Oh, there is so much rich meaning and beauty in the art of the ages for you who have eyes to see!

Upon my short visit to this temple of art I should not be able to review a fraction of that great world of art which is open to you. I should be able to get only a superficial impression. Artists tell me that for a deep and true appreciation of art one must educate the eye. One must learn from experience to weigh the merits of line, of composition, of form and color. If I had eyes, how happily would I embark upon so fascinating a study! Yet I am told that, to many of you who have eyes to see, the world of art is a dark night, unexplored and unilluminated.

It would be with extreme reluctance that I should leave the Metropolitan Museum, which contains the key to beauty - a beauty so neglected. Seeing persons, however, do not need a Metropolitan to find this key to beauty. The same key lies waiting in smaller museums, and in books on the shelves of even small libraries. But naturally, in my limited time of imaginary sight, I should choose the place where the key unlocks the greatest treasures in the shortest time.

The evening of my second day of sight I should spend at a theatre or at the movies. Even now I often attend theatrical performances of all sorts, but the action of the play must be spelled into my hand by a companion. But how I should like to see with my own eyes the fascinating figure of

Hamlet, or the gusty Falstaff amid colorful Elizabethan trappings! How I should like to follow each movement of the graceful Hamlet, each strut of the hearty Falstaff! And since I could see only one play, I should be confronted by a many-horned dilemma, for there are scores of plays I should want to see. You who have eyes can see any you like. How many of you, I wonder, when you gaze at a play, a movie, or any spectacle, realize and give thanks for the miracle of sight which enables you to enjoy its color, grace, and movement?

I cannot enjoy the beauty rythmic movement except in a sphere restricted to the touch of my hands. I can vision only dimly the grace of a Pavlowa, although I know something of the delight of rhythm, for often I can sense the beat of music as it vibrates through the floor. I can well imagine that cadenced motion must be one of the most pleasing sights in the world. I have been able to gather something of this by tracing with my fingers the lines in sculptured marble; if this static grace can be so lovely, how much more acute must be the thrill of seeing grace in motion.

One of my dearest memories is of the time when Joseph Jefferson allowed me to touch his face and hands as he went through some of the gestures and speeches of his beloved Rip Van Winkle. I was able to catch thus a meager glimpse of the world of drama, and I shall never forget the delight of that moment. But, oh, how much I must miss, and how much pleasure you seeing ones can derive from watching and hearing the interplay of speech and movement in

the unfolding of a dramatic per-
formance! If I could see only one
play, I should know how to picture in my mind the action of a
hundred plays which I have read
or had transferred to me through
the medium of manual alphabet.

So, through the evening of my
second imaginary day of sight, the
great figures of dramatic
literature would crowd sleep from
my eyes.

FOUR

The following morning, I should
again greet the dawn, anxious to
discover new delights, for I am
sure that, for those who have eyes
which really see, the dawn of each
day must be a perpetually new re-
velation of beauty.

This, according to the terms of my imagined miracle, is to be my third and last day of sight. I shall have no time to waste in regrets or longings; there is too much to see. The first day I devoted to my friends, animate and inanimate. The second revealed to me the history of man and Nature. To-day I shall spend in the workday world of the present, amid the haunts of men going about the business of life. And where one can find so many activities and conditions of men as in New York? So the city becomes my destination.

I start from my home in the quiet little suburb of Forest Hills, Long Island. Here, surrounded by green lawns, trees, and flowers, are neat little houses, happy with the voices and movements of wives and children, havens of peaceful rest for men who toil in the city. I drive across the lacy structure of steel which spans the East River, and I get a new and startling vision of the power and ingenuity of the mind of man. Busy boats chug and scurry about the river - racy speed, boats, stolid, snorting tugs. If I had long days of sight ahead, I should spend many of them watching the delightful activity upon the river.

I look ahead, and before me rise the fantastic towers of New York, a city that seems to have stepped from the pages of a fairy story. What an awe-inspiring sight, these glittering spires, these vast banks of stone and steel - sculptures such as the gods might build for themselves! This animated picture is a part of the lives of millions of people every day. How many, I wonder, give it so much as a second glance? Very few, I fear. Their eyes are blind to this magnificent sight because it is so familiar to them.

I hurry to the top of one of those gigantic structures, the Empire State Building, for there, a short time ago, I 'saw' the city below through the eyes of my secretary. I am anxious to compare my fancy with reality. I am sure I should not be disappointed in the panorama spread out before me, for to me it would be a vision of another world.

Now I begin my rounds of the city. First, I stand at a busy corner, merely looking at people, trying by sight of them to understand something of their lives. I see smiles, and I am happy. I see serious determination, and I am proud. I see suffering, and I am compassionate.

I stroll down Fifth Avenue. I throw my eyes out of focus, so that I see no particular object but a seething kaleidoscope of color. I am certain that the colors of women's dresses moving in a throng must be a gorgeous spectacle of which I should never tire. But perhaps if I had sight I should be like most other women - too interested in styles and the cut of individual dresses to give much attention to the splendor of color in the mass. And I am convinced, too, that I should become an inveterate window shopper, for it must be a delight to the eye to view the myriad articles of beauty on display.

From Fifth Avenue I make a tour of the city - to Park Avenue, to the slums, to factories, to parks

where children play. I take a stay-
at-home trip abroad by visiting
the foreign quarters. Always my
eyes are open wide to all the
sights of both happiness and mise-
ry so that I may probe deep and
add to my understanding of how
people work and live. My heart is
full of the images of people and
things. My eye passes lightly over
no single trifle; it strives to touch
and hold closely each thing its
gaze rests upon. Some sights are
pleasant, filling the heart with
happiness; but some are miserably
pathetic. To these latter I do not
shut my eyes, for they, too are
part of life. To close the eye on
them is to close the heart and
mind.

My third day of sight is draw-
ing to an end. Perhaps there are
many serious pursuits to which I
should devote the few remaining

hours, but I am afraid that on the
evening of that last day I should
run away to the theatre, to a hi-
lariously funny play, so that I
might appreciate the overtones of
comedy in the human spirit.

At midnight my temporary respite
from blindness would cease, and
permanent night would close in on
me again. Naturally in those three
short days I should not have seen
all I wanted to see. Only when
darkness had again descended upon
me should I realize how much I had
left unseen. But my mind would be
so overcrowded with glorious memories that I should have little time
for regrets. Thereafter the touch of
every object would bring a glowing
memory of how that object looked.

Perhaps this short outline of
how I should spend three days of
sight does not agree with the pro-

gramme you would set for your-
self if you knew that you were
about to be stricken blind. I am,
however, sure that if you actually faced that fate your eyes would
open to things you had never seen
before, storing up memories for
the long night ahead. You would
use your eyes as never before.
Everything you saw would become
dear to you. Your eyes would
touch and embrace every object
that came within your range of
vision. Then, at last, you would
really see, and a new world of
beauty would open itself before
you.

I who am blind can give one
hint to those who see - one admo-
nition to those who would make
full use of the gift of sight: Use
your eyes as if tomorrow you
would be stricken blind. And the
same method can be applied to

other senses. Hear the music of voices, the song of a bird, the mighty strains of an orchestra, as if you would be stricken deaf tomorrow. Touch each object you want to touch as if tomorrow your tactile sense would fail. Smell the perfume of flowers, taste with relish each morsel, as if tomorrow you could never smell and taste again. Make the most of every sense; glory in all the facets of pleasure and beauty which the world reveals to you through the several means of contact which Nature provides. But of all the senses, I am sure that sight must be the most delightful.

~~~~~~

Helen Keller Handwriting Font

is available here:

etsy.com/uk/shop/UnschoolarHealingHub

~~~~~~

To get this **Notebook with 64 Helen Keller Quotes in Helen Keller Handwriting Font,** see amazon or this website:

~~~~~~

Printed in Great Britain
by Amazon